941 05

Clothes

Peter Chrisp

Wayland

Titles in the series

Clothes

Country Life

Exploration

Food

Homes

Kings and Queens

Life at Sea

Religion

Scientists and Writers

Town Life

Cover illustrations: *background* The christening of Henry VII's son, Prince Arthur, 1486; *inset* miniature of a young man leaning against a rose tree, about 1588.

First published in 1994 by Wayland (Publishers) Ltd
61 Western Road, Hove, East Sussex, BN3 1JD, England

Editor: Cath Senker
Designer: John Christopher
Picture researcher: Elizabeth Moore

British Library Cataloguing in Publication Data
Peter Chrisp
Clothes. – (Tudors and Stuarts series)
I. Title II. Series
391.0091

ISBN 0-7502-1151-2

Typeset by Strong Silent Type
Printed and bound by B.P.C.C. Paulton Books, Great Britain

Picture acknowledgements

Ashmolean Museum, Oxford 18 (above), 21 (above); Bridgeman *cover* (inset), (Guildhall Art Gallery) 4, (Belvoir Castle, Leics) 8, 9 (above), 11 (both; below from Victoria and Albert Museum), (York City Art Gallery) 13 (above), (G Roberton) 15, 24, 26 (above); The Matthews Collection, Chertsey Museum 18 (below); Edinburgh University Library 17 (both); E.T. Archive *title page*, 6, 21 (below); Fotomas *cover* (background), 7 (below), 9 (below), 16, 25, 26 (below); Mary Evans Picture Library 5 (both), 7 (above), 19, 27; Trustees of the National Library of Scotland 20; National Portrait Gallery 10, 23; National Trust (P A Burton) 14; Tate Gallery 13 (below), 22 (both; below by J Webb); Weiss Gallery 12.

Notes for teachers

Clothes draws on a wide range of exciting sources, including paintings, artefacts, drawings and quotations. This book:

◆ explains how you can learn about people's status and lifestyle from the clothes they wore;

◆ looks at the laws decreeing what kinds of clothes different classes in society were allowed to wear, and gives examples of people who broke the rules;

◆ shows how fashions were influenced by the clothes worn by the royal family and how changes in fashion filtered down through the rest of society;

◆ looks at the changing fashions of men and women during the period;

◆ examines the materials used to make clothes and the skills involved;

◆ describes the clothes worn in Ireland and Scotland;

◆ shows how babies and children were dressed;

◆ helps the reader to understand how to use clues from the past to learn about how people lived in Tudor and Stuart times.

Contents

What do clothes tell us?

Sir William Craven in 1611. His gold chain shows us that he is Lord Mayor.

This book is about the sort of clothes worn by British people during the time of the Tudors and Stuarts. The Tudors were a family of kings and queens who ruled England, Wales and Ireland from 1485 to 1603. The Stuarts, who also ruled Scotland, were in power from 1603 to 1714.

Just like today, in Tudor and Stuart times you could tell a lot about people from their clothes. This painting shows the Lord Mayor of London wearing a long thick robe. Robes like this were worn by lawyers and merchants, people who spent long hours sitting down at their work. They needed robes to keep warm, for buildings then were cold and draughty.

The long robe was also a sign of 'respectability', like a suit is today. By wearing a robe, a man showed other people that he was of a higher class than a labourer.

On the right is the kind of outfit worn by people who worked with their hands. This man is a blacksmith. Unlike Sir William, blacksmiths did not need to dress for warmth. Their place of work was hot and the hard work made them hotter still.

The blacksmith wears clothes that allow him to bend and move freely. They are close fitting, but not so tight that they are uncomfortable. Everything he wears is practical.

(Above) A drawing of a blacksmith, 1647.

Now look at this rich couple. Their clothes are puffed out and decorated with feathers and lace. These were the sort of clothes worn by courtiers, people who spent their days with the king or queen. None of the clothes were practical. People wore them to show how rich and fashionable they were.

A fashionable couple, around 1600.

The laws and customs of clothes

Below is a picture of King Henry VIII with his jester (clown), Will Summers. Even if you have never seen a picture of Henry before, you can tell by the clothes which man is which. While Will's clothes are plain, Henry's are richly decorated with gold. If Will had tried dressing like Henry, he would have been breaking the law.

Henry VIII and his jester.

In Henry's time, there were laws which said what sort of clothes you were allowed to wear. Only members of the royal family could dress in cloth of gold. No one below the rank of baron could wear cloth of silver.

There were even laws which said how much labourers were allowed to spend on their hose (leggings). A labourer caught wearing hose costing more than tenpence a yard could be locked up for three days!

The reason for these laws was that Henry and his government believed that everyone had a natural place in society, decided by God. Your clothes were a sign of your place. The richer your clothes, the higher up you must be. They thought that it was wrong to rise above your level in society by wearing expensive clothes.

As well as breaking the law, you could upset people by dressing in certain ways. For one thing, people have always expected women and men to dress differently. However, in the early 1600s, there was a woman in London called Mary Frith, who dressed as a man and smoked a pipe. For most Londoners, this behaviour was really shocking. Mary was so unusual that she had a play written about her, *The Roaring Girl*.

A drawing from 1611 showing **Mary Frith** smoking a pipe and holding a sword.

(Below) Two pictures of Nicholas Gennings, who shocked people in Elizabethan times by wearing different disguises to go begging.

At the court of Henry VIII

The biggest influence on fashion was the royal family. When the king or queen changed hairstyle or clothes, the courtiers would copy the new style. In turn, the courtiers were copied by wealthy people throughout the land.

King Henry VIII was a huge man, 1.9 m tall, and very heavy. He wore clothes that made him look broad and strong rather than fat. Until Henry's time, most Englishmen used to shave. Henry changed this by growing a beard to hide his double chin. Suddenly beards became fashionable.

Look at Henry in this portrait. His thick cloak and massive padded shoulders are designed to make him look strong. Everything about him seems square-shaped – even the toes of his shoes.

A portrait of Henry VIII by the painter Hans Holbein.

The women of Henry's court dressed to look beautiful. In Henry's time, this meant appearing small and delicate. This is Jane Seymour, Henry's third wife. Her hair is hidden under a 'gable hood' – named after the edge of a roof, which is what it looks like. You can see that the top part of her dress, the bodice, is stiff and tight. It must have made it difficult to breathe.

(Right) Jane Seymour, painted by Holbein.

On the left is a full-length view of the sort of dress worn by Jane Seymour. The dress ends in a long 'train', which drags along the ground. Women could not move about very quickly or easily in clothes like these. They weren't expected to. The women of Henry's court moved slowly and gracefully.

This drawing from about 1540 shows two views of the same woman wearing a dress with a long train.

1509
Henry VIII becomes king.

1530s
Beards and short hair become popular for men.

1536
Henry marries Jane Seymour.

1547
Death of Henry VIII.

Changing fashions: men

After King Henry VIII's time, many changes took place in the clothing of noblemen. The noblemen often copied the clothes worn in other countries, especially in Spain, France and Italy.

They spent huge sums keeping up with the latest fashions. It was expensive to stay just a week at the court of the king or queen. Nobody wanted to be seen wearing the same clothes twice.

This painting of Robert Dudley, Earl of Leicester, shows what rich men were wearing in the 1570s. Dudley's doublet (jacket) is padded out with stuffing. This stuffing was called 'bombast'. He also has stuffing in his trunk hose (short leggings), which swell out below his waist. The doublet is slashed to show the lining.

Around his neck, Dudley is wearing a white ruff. This was a new fashion. It was only made possible in the 1560s, when English people learned how to stiffen material with starch.

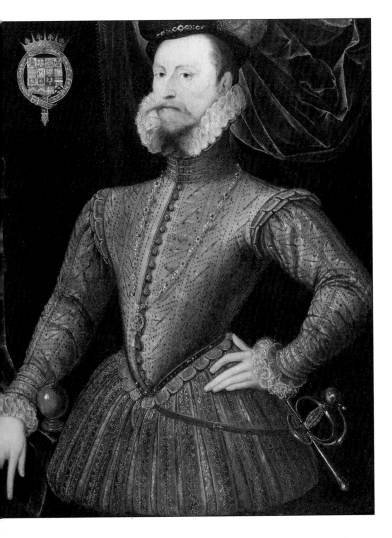

Robert Dudley's clothes are heavily padded to make it look as if he has a tiny waist. This fashion would never have caught on under Henry VIII.

(Above) An unnamed young man leaning against a rose tree.

The painting above shows men's clothes in about 1588. You can see that the ruff has got much bigger and the doublet is even more puffed out. It juts out in front of the belly, and is called a 'peascod'.

11

Some people thought that such doublets were ridiculous and made fun of them. Here is how one writer, Philip Stubbes, described them in 1583:

"Their doublets are monstrous, for now the fashion is to hang them down to the middle of the thighs, being so hard quilted and stuffed, bombasted and sewed, as they can hardly bend down."

(Below) Footwear had its own fashions. Look at the shoes worn in the early 1600s by Richard Sackville, Earl of Dorset.

1540s

Men start wearing baggy trunk hose on top of their long hose (stockings).

1560s

Men and women start wearing starched ruffs.

1570s

Men's clothes become heavily padded with bombast.

Changing fashions: women

Women's fashions changed just as much as men's in the Tudor and Stuart period. Like the men's doublets, women's dresses became more padded, with puffed-out sleeves. The skirt grew wider, held out by a bum roll (cloth padding) or by a farthingale – a framework of hoops made from wood, wire or whalebone.

In the 1550s, women wore a Spanish farthingale, which was shaped like a bell. Later, in the 1570s, they started wearing a French farthingale, which stuck straight out from the waist. Like the ruff, the farthingale got bigger and bigger. In the end, it was difficult for women wearing them to go through doorways.

This woman, Mary Fitton, was painted in about 1600 wearing a wide French farthingale. The top of her dress has a long stiffened front called a 'stomacher'.

Like most wealthy women of the time, Mary Fitton is wearing make-up. Her face and neck have been whitened, using egg-whites or white lead. She has reddened her lips and cheeks with cochineal, paint made from crushed beetles.

Can you find the insects made from pearls on Mary Fitton's dress?

It took a long time for rich women to get dressed in the morning, even with the help of their maids. A writer called Thomas Tomkins described some of the things that had to be done:

> *"There is such doing with their looking-glasses, pinning, unpinning, painting blue veins and cheeks; such stir with combs, necklaces, fans; such a calling for farthingales, shoe ties etc. A ship is sooner rigged by far than a gentlewoman made ready."*

(Above) Lady Frances Fairfax, painted in the early 1600s. She wears a lace collar, held in place by fine wire.

(Left) Lady Kitson in outdoor clothes, painted in 1573. Her hat is decorated with an expensive ostrich feather.

Timeline

1550s
Women start wearing the bell-shaped Spanish farthingale.

1570s
Women start wearing the wider French farthingale.

13

Queen Elizabeth I

In the 1500s, nobody spent more on clothes than Queen Elizabeth. In this painting, made when she was 59, you can see just one of the hundreds of dresses she owned.

From the tips of her shoes to the top of her wig, Elizabeth is covered in pearls and precious stones. Her dress, embroidered with whales and sea monsters, is held out by a huge French farthingale. Imagine what it would be like to walk about in such an outfit!

Queen Elizabeth in about 1592.

A painting of Queen Elizabeth dancing with Robert Dudley, Earl of Leicester.

Surprisingly, not only did Elizabeth walk about in such outfits every day, she even danced in them. The queen loved dancing. In this second painting you can see her being swept into the air as she takes part in one of the most popular dances, *la volta*. It may be that Elizabeth's farthingale has special metal handles to help her partner to lift her.

Elizabeth dressed like this to impress people, especially important foreign visitors. Paul Hentzner was a German who saw the queen in 1598. This is how he described her:

"*Next came the Queen, in the sixty-fifth year of her age (as we were told), very majestic; her face oblong, fair but wrinkled; her nose a little hooked, and her teeth black. She had in her ears two pearls with very rich drops. Her hair was of an auburn colour, but false.*

"*Her bosom was uncovered, as all the English ladies have it till they marry; and she had on a necklace of exceedingly fine jewels. That day she was dressed in white silk bordered with pearls of the size of beans, and over it a mantle of black silk shot with silver threads.*"

Working people

Keeping up with the latest fashions was only for the rich. The drawing below from 1592 shows the difference between a fashionable town gentleman, called 'velvet breeches', and a man from the countryside, called 'cloth breeches'. The fashionable man wears clothes decorated with many buttons, a wide ruff and a hat with ostrich feathers. The countryman has a plain outfit of simple russet – coarse woollen cloth, spun at home. His whole outfit would have been made by one of the women in his family.

A drawing of a rich townsman and a poor countryman.

A working woman wasn't interested in fancy clothes like farthingales, even if she could have afforded them. She would wear a simple dress, an apron and often a square of cloth around her neck called a neckerchief.

(Right) This sketch, made in 1614, shows a farmer and his wife bringing goods to market.

Some changes in fashion did eventually reach poorer people, like the farmer and his wife above. As well as wearing practical clothes, such as an apron, the woman above is wearing a small ruff. The farmer is wearing short trunk hose, a simpler version of the puffed-out leggings worn by the fashionable men on pages 10–11. Of course, as soon as ordinary people started wearing these things, they went right out of fashion.

This blind water carrier wears loose hose. They are like trunk hose but they are not padded. This must be one of the earliest pictures of a guide dog.

Making clothes

In Tudor and Stuart times, all clothes were made by hand. The commonest and cheapest material was wool, from English sheep. Wool could be spun to make many different sorts of fabric, from coarse russet to soft velvet. All kinds of clothes were made from wool.

The second most common material was linen, which came from the flax plant. Linen was used for shirts and underwear. The most expensive materials of all were cotton and silk, because they were produced overseas.

A pair of white leather gloves, embroidered with gold thread. They were given to Queen Elizabeth in 1566.

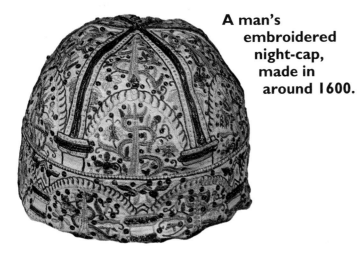

A man's embroidered night-cap, made in around 1600.

Most people wore clothes made at home, by the women of the family. Even in rich houses, women made simple clothing, such as shirts and caps. Often such women were servants, but even the wealthiest women liked doing embroidery. They used coloured silks and silver and gold thread to make pictures of flowers, animals and insects. Embroidery was used to decorate all items of clothing, even shoes and hats.

Tailors at work in 1659.

Tailors, who were always men, made fashionable clothes for wealthy people. Tailoring was a highly-skilled craft and tailors were supposed to belong to organizations called guilds. These made sure that work was of a certain standard; guilds could fine members who made faulty clothes.

To become a tailor, a boy had to spend a long time as an apprentice. He learned how to measure a customer and how to cut expensive cloth, like silk, without wasting any.

Tailors had to keep in touch with the latest fashions. One place they could do this was St. Paul's Church in London. Every morning, young men paraded up and down the middle of St. Paul's showing off their latest outfits. Tailors hid behind the columns, taking notes on what was 'in' and what was 'out'. It was just like a modern fashion show.

Scottish and Irish clothes

A Highland woman
in about 1610 wearing
a plaid.

Some parts of the British Isles had their own separate ways of dressing. In Ireland and in the Highlands of Scotland, people went barefoot and wrapped themselves in long woollen blankets. In Ireland, this blanket was plain brown and was called a 'mantle' (cloak). The Scots called their blanket a 'plaid'. Unlike the mantle, the plaid was woven in bright tartan patterns. The Scots used plants, such as lichen, to make colourful dyes.

The English thought that the Scots and Irish were backward people who dressed in strange outfits. They called them 'wild Irish' and 'wild Scots' and 'red shanks' (red legs). Henry VIII even passed laws to make Irish people dress like English people. The Irish ignored these laws.

In fact, the blankets were practical dress for the wet and cold weather of Scotland and Ireland. The Irish mantle, for example, was skilfully woven and then combed to give it a thick, curly nap (surface). This made it warm and waterproof. Going barefoot was also sensible in wet and boggy places.

Fynes Morison was an Englishman who travelled to Ireland in the 1600s. He described how useful the mantle was to an Irishman:

> " *When it raineth, it is his home; when it bloweth, it is his tent. In summer, he can wear it loose; in winter he can wrap it close.* "

(Above) A copy of a picture of Irish soldiers drawn in the 1540s. They wear long mantles and are barefoot.

Rich English people loved to wear strange costumes for masques, which were like fancy-dress parties. On the left is Thomas Lee, a wealthy Englishman who served as a soldier in Ireland. He is wearing a fancy-dress version of traditional Irish costume. It is very different from what Irish people really wore. No ordinary Irishman would have worn a shirt as richly decorated as this.

Thomas Lee, an Englishman dressed as an Irishman, painted in 1594.

Children's clothes

This is a painting of the Cholmondeley twins, sisters who had been married on the same day and who also gave birth on the same day. They are sitting up in bed, showing off their new babies. The babies are swaddled (wrapped up) in bandages. For hundreds of years, British babies were tightly swaddled like this.

(Above) A seventeenth-century painting of the Cholmondeley sisters and their babies.

When children grew big enough to walk, they were put into dresses – boys as well as girls. Here is another painting celebrating the birth of a new baby. It shows the Saltonstall family in 1637. One of the children on the left is a boy. Can you tell which one?

The Saltonstall family.

It was a big moment in every boy's life when, at about the age of eight, he was breeched – given his first pair of men's breeches (trousers). In this painting, you can see eight-year-old Wat Raleigh, standing beside his father, the explorer Sir Walter Raleigh. Wat is dressed like a small grown-up. He even has a sword.

The children in these paintings were all from rich families and they were wearing their best clothes for the occasion. Their everyday wear may well have been plainer and simpler. Poorer children would have dressed even more simply in clothes made at home. Poor boys wore slops (loose trousers). Girls wore simple dresses and aprons, just like their mothers.

Sir Walter Raleigh and his son, painted in 1602.

Puritans

Puritans were people with strict ideas about religion, ideas which affected the way that they dressed. They believed that it was sinful, or wicked, to show off by wearing expensive and fashionable clothes.

Puritans thought that it was wrong to wear anything that might make you feel proud of your appearance. They said that people should dress as simply as possible. The men wore plain white shirts and dark jackets, and had their hair cut short.

The women wore brown or black dresses and jackets. They covered their heads with plain white bonnets (small hats) and tall dark hats in a shape called a 'sugar loaf'.

Catherine Davenant, a Puritan, wearing a sugar-loaf hat.

Some Puritans even refused to wear buttons, because they thought they looked too fancy.

The drawing on the left from the 1640s shows all the things that Puritans hated. This fashionable young man is covered in ribbons. He has long hair, also tied with ribbons, and he is wearing make-up – 'patches', or beauty spots. His boots are much longer than his feet.

Some rich people were influenced by Puritan ideas about clothes. They began to wear darker colours and use linen instead of lace for colours and cuffs. However, they found that they could dress simply but still look impressive. They wore black silk and expensive linen from Holland.

A fashionable man in 1646.

25

Men in wigs

The return of King Charles II in 1660 had a great effect on the way men dressed. Charles had been living abroad in France – he had been forced to flee there during the wars between his father, Charles I, and the English Parliament. When Charles II came back in 1660, he was wearing a long, full wig. The wig had been made fashionable in France by King Louis XIII, who was bald.

(Above) A painting of Robert Kerr, Earl of Lothian in 1667, wearing one of the new wigs made popular by King Charles II.

(Below) Wearing his wig, Charles II rides off to be crowned king.

Samuel Pepys was a wealthy man who wanted to try out the new periwigs, as they were called. In May 1663, he wrote in his diary:

> "*At Mr Jervas's, my old barber, I did try two or three periwigs, meaning to wear one; and yet I have no stomach for it.*"

It wasn't until November that Pepys finally found the courage to buy a wig. In order to wear it, he had to have his own hair cut off (it was taken away to make another wig). When he got home, Pepys asked his maids their opinion.

They liked the wig, but they were shocked to learn that he had had his hair cut off.

Pepys then went to church, expecting everyone to stare and point at him. To his relief, they didn't. His wig was there to stay.

A seventeenth-century wig maker.

1624

King Louis XIII of France, who is bald, starts wearing a wig. Wigs become fashionable in France.

1642–49

English Civil War.

1660

Charles Stuart crowned as King Charles II. Wigs become fashionable in Britain.

1660s

Fashionable men start wearing wigs and long coats.

Timeline

1480	1500	1520	1540	1560	1580

Tudors

1485 HENRY VII

1509 HENRY VIII

1547 EDWARD VI
1553 MARY TUDOR
1558 ELIZABETH I

1480–1500	1500–1520	1520–1540	1540–1560	1560–1580	1580–1600

1480–1500

1480
Men begin to grow their hair long and are clean-shaven.

1485
The Battle of Bosworth ends the Wars of the Roses.

1492
Christopher Columbus sails to the West Indies.

1499
Amerigo Vespucci's first voyage to America.

1500–1520

1500–1547
Sheep farmers enclose common land.

1507
Amerigo Vespucci's name is given to America.

1510
A new law states what kinds of clothes people of different social classes are allowed to wear.

1515
Cardinal Wolsey becomes Lord Chancellor.

1517
Martin Luther leads the Protestant Reformation in Germany.

1520–1540

1520
The Spanish start to colonize the American mainland.

1530s
Fashionable men grow beards and have their hair cut short.

1534
Henry VIII makes himself Head of the Church in England.

1536–39
Henry VIII has the monasteries destroyed.

1540–1560

1547–53
Many new schools and colleges are founded.

1553–58
Many Protestants are persecuted and put to death under Queen Mary.

1554
Queen Mary marries King Philip of Spain. Spanish fashions become popular in England. Women wear the Spanish farthingale under their dresses.

1560–1580

1560–80
Curly hair becomes fashionable for men. Men and women start wearing ruffs.

1567
Mary Queen of Scots flees to England but is imprisoned by Queen Elizabeth.

1577
Francis Drake sets off on his voyage around the world.

1580–1600

1580–1600
The wider French farthingale replaces the Spanish farthingale.

1584
Tobacco and potatoes are first brought to England by Sir Walter Raleigh.

1587
Mary Queen of Scots is executed.

1588
The Spanish Armada is defeated by the English fleet.

1590s
Shoulder-length hair becomes fashionable for men.

1590–1616
William Shakespeare writes his plays.

1600   1620   1640   1660   1680   1700

Stuarts

1603 JAMES I
(JAMES VI OF
SCOTLAND)

1625 CHARLES I

1649–1660 COMMONWEALTH
1653 OLIVER CROMWELL
1658 RICHARD CROMWELL

1660 CHARLES II

1685 JAMES II
1688 WILLIAM III & MARY II

1702–1714 ANNE

1600–1620	1620–1640	1640–1660	1660–1680	1680–1700	1700–1720
1601 The Poor Law provides help for poor people. **1603** The English and Scottish crowns are united in the Stuart King James. **1603–42** Fashions become simpler and more comfortable. Ruffs go out of fashion. Rich women wear loose satin dresses. **1605** The Gunpowder Plot.	**1620** The Pilgrim Fathers sail to America. **1628** William Harvey describes how the blood goes around the body. **1629–1640** Charles I rules without Parliament.	**1640** The Scots defeat Charles I. **1642–49** Civil war between King Charles and Parliament. Fighting for Parliament are many Puritans who dress simply and have short hair. They are nicknamed 'roundheads'. **1649** Charles I is put to death. **1653–58** Oliver Cromwell rules as Lord Protector.	**1660** The monarchy is restored with Charles II. **1660–69** Samuel Pepys writes his diary. **1660s** Charles II introduces French fashions to English men, in particular coats, waistcoats and wigs. **1665** The Great Plague. **1666** The Great Fire of London.	**1688** William III and Mary II are crowned. James II flees England. **1690** James II is defeated by William III at the Battle of the Boyne in Ireland. **1694** Queen Mary dies.	**1707** The kingdoms of England and Scotland are officially united. **1714** The Stuart period ends with the death of Queen Anne. George I becomes the first Hanoverian king.

Glossary

Apprentice Someone who works for a skilled person for several years to learn a craft.

Blacksmith A skilled person who makes and mends articles of iron.

Bodice The upper part of a woman's dress.

Bombast Padding made from horsehair, cotton or wool.

Doublet A man's close-fitting jacket.

Farthingale A series of hoops, made from wood, bone, or wire, worn under a skirt to make it stick out.

Hose A man's leg coverings, similar to tights.

Lace A delicate fabric made of cotton, silk, linen or wool threads and woven into patterns.

Linen Material made from the flax plant.

Peascod A heavily-padded doublet, worn by men in the 1580s and 1590s.

Puritan Someone who lives and dresses as simply as possible, for religious reasons.

Ruff A frill worn around the neck, made of folds of starched linen or cotton.

Russet Coarse woollen cloth, spun at home.

Silk A fine, soft material, made from the fibre produced by silkworms.

Trunk hose Men's short, puffed-out leggings, worn on top of hose. They swelled outwards from the waist and usually ended at the thigh.

Velvet A soft fabric, originally woven from silk. Cheaper velvet was made from cotton or wool.

Books to read

Besson, Jean-Louis *Clothes Through the Ages* (Moonlight Publishers, 1988)
Clarke, Suzy (Ed.) *Tudor Clothes* (Young Library, 1989
Morley, Jacqueline *Clothes* (Franklin Watts, 1992)

Ralph Lewis, Brenda *Clothes* (Wayland, 1988)
Tarrant, Naomi *Costume in Scotland Through the Ages* (Chambers, 1991)
Wright, Rachel *Tudors* (Franklin Watts, 1993)
Wright, Rachel *Stuarts* (Franklin Watts, 1993)

Places to visit

You can see examples of Tudor and Stuart clothes in museums. Here are the main ones:

The Costume Museum Nottingham, 51 Castle Gate, Nottingham NG1 6AF; tel. 0602 483504.
The Gallery of English Costume Manchester City Art Galleries, Platt Hall, off Oxford Rd, Manchester; tel. 061 224 5217.
The Museum of Costume Bennett St, Bath; tel. 0225 461111.
The Museum of Leathercraft 60 Bridge St, Northampton NN1 1PA; tel. 0604 601453.
The Museum of London Barbican, London; tel. 071 600 3699.
The Victoria and Albert Museum South Kensington, London SW7 2RL; tel. 071 938 8500.

Other museums with some clothes in their collections:

Museum of Birmingham Chamberlain Square, Birmingham B3 3DH; tel. 021 235 2834.
National Museums of Scotland Chambers St, Edinburgh EH1 1JF; tel. 031 225 7534.
Welsh Folk Museum National Museum of Wales, St Fagan's, near Cardiff; tel. 0222 569441.
The National Portrait Gallery St Martin's Place, London WC2H OHE; tel. 071 306 0055. Has paintings showing Tudor and Stuart clothes.

Index

Words in **bold** are subjects shown in pictures as well as in the text.